NIGHTS AT THE MUSEUM

or the Fabulist Adventures in Tartu, Estonia
of the Old Man from Kentucky
and His Familiars

"We all know that Art is not truth.
Art is a lie that makes us realize truth,
at least the truth that is given us to understand."
Pablo Picasso

OTHER BOOKS
BY JINN BUG & RON WHITEHEAD

Disobey

OTHER BOOKS BY RON WHITEHEAD

A Taoist Nun Teaches Me in Fourteen Poems

Beaver Dam Rocking Chair Marathon

blistered asphalt on dixie highway: Kentucky Basketball Is Poetry in Motion

Blood Filled Vessels Racing to the Heart

EVE & The OPHIDIANS

Ghost Lover, Trance Mission

I'd Never Shoot a Man While He's Washing Dishes: Arcturian Love Songs

I Refuse I Will Not Bow Down I Will Never Give Up

I Will Not Bow Down

Kentucky Bound: poems, stories & songs

Kokopelli

Mama: a poet's heart in a Kentucky girl, photo edition

MAMA: a poet's heart in a Kentucky Girl

Quest for Self in the Ocean of Consciousness: Ibsen, Hamsun, Munch, Joyce

Searching for Jack Kerouac

The Declaration of Independence This Time: Selected Poems

The Path of the Ancient Skald

The Storm Generation: Poems by Outlaw Poet Ron Whitehead

The Storm Generation Manifesto & On Parting

The Third Testament: Three Gospels of Peace

The View from Lawrence Ferlinghetti's Bathroom Window

The Wanderer

We See the Sound of Setting Sun

Western Kentucky: Lost & Forgotten, Found & Remembered

AUDIO RECORDINGS
BY RON WHITEHEAD

Down & Out in Kentucky: Never Give Up

DRAGONS

Exterminate Noise

Frogg Corpse & Mr. Stranger Present the End of the World

From Iceland to Kentucky & Beyond

I Refuse

I Will Not Bow Down

Kentucky Blues

Kentucky Roots

Kentucky: poems, stories, songs

Pack My Soul in Dry Ice

Prayer

Riding with Rebel Jesus

Ron Whitehead and Southside's Southside Lounge

Ron Whitehead and Southside's We Are the Storm double-CD

Searching for Jack Kerouac

Songs & Poems from the Kentucky Bound Concert

Swan Boats @ Four

Tapping My Own Phone

The Bonemen

The Dance

The Shape of Water

The Storm Generation Manifesto & On Parting, the Wilderness Poems

The Storm Generation Manifesto & Other Rock n Roll Poems

The Viking Hillbilly Apocalypse Revue

Trance Mission

Walking Home

Whirlpool

NIGHTS AT THE MUSEUM

or the Fabulist Adventures in Tartu, Estonia
of the Old Man from Kentucky
and His Familiars

TRANCEMISSION PRESS

Historic Clarksville, Indiana

Trancemission Press
301 S Clark Blvd
Clarksville IN 47129
www.trancemission.xyz

**Nights at the Museum or the Fabulist Adventures in Tartu,
Estonia of the Old Man from Kentucky and His Familiars
Jinn Bug & Ron Whitehead**
1st edition
ISBN- 9781075606298

Foreword

In 2019, Ron Whitehead was named Writer in Residence for the UNESCO City of Literature international residency program in Tartu, Estonia and invited to spend April and May 2019 living in the Karl Ristikivi Muuseum in Tartu. When he arrived, he had no intention of writing a book of poems about Estonia. He had resolved to use the gift of the residency to finish his manuscript THE VIEW FROM LAWRENCE FERLINGHETTI'S BATHROOM WINDOW: Poems, Stories, Interviews, Photos: From The Beat to The Underground, and to edit HUNTER S. THOMPSON'S HELL'S ANGELS: Writers & Editors, Romance & Trouble by Margaret Ann Harrell. He also eagerly anticipated helping coordinate Estonia's first Insomniacathon—a 24 hour nonstop poetry and music performance to conclude Tartu's 2019 International Prima Vista Literature Festival.

Since he was young, Ron has had wanderlust and simultaneously experiences profound homesickness immediately upon leaving. To help distract him from missing home as he adjusted to complete immersion in Estonia and to challenge him to get out and about, Ron's partner in art and life—Jinn Bug—suggested he take long walks and write a daily poem about what he saw and experienced. Ron's first poem—which does not appear in this manuscript—was raw and painful. Jinn invented a device—the adventures of an old man and an imaginary boy in Estonia—and suggested creating a series of fairytale-like storied poems that explore the folklore, myth, politics and culture of Estonia while simultaneously capturing a bit of the poets' own human experiences. Separated by 5,000 miles and a seven hour time difference, the two poets visited daily with each other via

Facebook video calls and in the body of this manuscript. In late April 2019, Jinn joined Ron for ten days in Estonia.

The poems in this book were born out of research, reading, and personal experience, enriched by contacts made and friendships formed by Ron during his time as Writer in Residence. The poems were also enlivened by mutual puzzling over and attempting to explain and understand things that were foreign to us.

Simple questions such as "What to do with my trash in Estonia?" and "What is up with this stupid coffee machine?" challenged creative minds to supply answers and explanations (see *The Ogre's Lunch*, *The Illusion of Choice*). Trying to wrap our hearts around what it might feel like to experience genocide and atrocity, occupation, war and exile influenced other poems in the book, including *Words Worth Dying For*, *Homeland*, and *The Ghost of Karl Ristikivi*. Other poems are our humble attempt to share the flavor of the history and culture of Estonia (*Soup Town Days*, *The Cathedral of Crows*). Still others explore our experiences of love and longing and loss and the phenomenon of aging in body while growing ever more unguarded and full of wonder inside (*When Everything Blossoms*, *On the Terrible Loneliness of Heroes*, *The Field Guide*).

The Afterword contains more information about our process of writing these poems and some hints as to which poet wrote what.

The old man who wanders the pages of this book is both Ron and is not Ron. The boy who travels with the old man is both imaginary and real; he embodies both poets' childlikeness and can access delight and ancient wisdom in ways grown folks forget. The woman who loves flowers is both Jinn and is not Jinn. Other characters who appear in this book are loosely or closely based on actual Estonians while a few are completely symbolic inventions.

There are both endangered tiny flying squirrels in Estonia and foxy red squirrels, but no gray squirrels such as the ones which chatter in "Taking Out the Trash." Wolves and hedgehogs and Rat Kings all exist in Estonia, as do werewolves, wizards, wise women, black storks and over 330 other species of birds.

It is impossible for two travelers to capture the rich culture, history, and spirit of a country and its people in a slim book of verse. Our hope is that these 31 poemed stories will entertain, provoke and—more importantly—encourage others to learn about and dream of a fabulous place that transcends time and space, that encompasses myth and history, and which symbolizes for us the freedom song of an oppressed yet resilient and triumphant nation: Eesti Vabariik, the Republic of Estonia.

Jinn Bug and Ron Whitehead

CONTENTS

Blessed Are the Innocent

Jesus said, *No prophet*
is accepted in his hometown,
something the old man mutters
aloud to no one and everyone
as he boards a plane to Estonia.

He is traveling to a country
no one back home has ever heard of;
his backpack contains one spangled suit
and all the books he's written
no one back home has ever read.

Goodbye, goodbye.

Just below him, someone weaves
roses into a garland for a winning nag
and the rich men who name laureates
stagger in a bourbon-gold afternoon.

The boy strokes the old man's whiskers
and whispers, "Remember,
it is a great honor to leave,
such a very great honor."
Blessed are the innocent.

Temporal Nonlocality

After a ten-hour delay in Chicago,
the old man is wired and sleepless.
He peers 35,000 feet down into darkness,
imagining the moaning jet's port and starboard
lights skittering across the sky, reflected
faint as stars in the faceless Atlantic Ocean.

How is it possible to see nothing in every direction
and still trust there are waves below and they sparkle
red and green in the waning crescent moon's light?
Perhaps the last seventy years have been
an extended practical joke, a laughable exercise
wrestling a clockwork cloak onto quantum chaos.

He looks at the boy sleeping beside him,
the boy he's known since he was a boy himself.
Here is an organism, overwhelmed by sensation,
bombarded with input, dosed with dream and
drunk with longing for significance. He pulls the
disposable blanket closer 'round the boy's shoulders,
rests his own bony cheek against the cold window
watching nothing stream by at 500 miles per hour,
still believing everything is possible.

On Luck and Magic

When she is sure the old man has nodded off in the broken
rusted blue chair he's dragged into the no moon's dark
outside the locked door of the museum, the prophetess En
whistles the boy over through a gap in the wooded palisade
that circles the building. She knows each of the 109 languages
spoken in Estonia but leaves speaking English to her grandson
who works nights as a ferryman and holds the key
to the museum's door. The boy is cold and lonesome.
He is certain their luck has run out under this starless sky.

The boy looks at En's moss-bloom whiskers
then he falls deep into her cavern dark eyes.
When she motions upward his gaze rises just above her head
where he sees a magical tree, one gnarled, twisted trunk
bearing apricots and nectarines and peaches and plums.
En knows what he is staring at and her knotted fingers
decode the mystery. She pantomimes biting an apple,
plucking a seed, tucking it in to the earth and then
an apple tree shooting up, up, up straight and true.

Her hands weave a storm and the apple tree breaks,
crown crashing down. The boy looks back to her face
and sees a little girl considering him, her arm cradling
boughs of many trees, one hand holding a knife.
He knows that she will cut the apple tree over and over
and in each wound she will snug a new branch,
watering the clefts with willow water so the rootstock
will sigh and accept the new sprigs as its own.

Not magic at all, her old-again brown eyes say,
Just hard work and time, my boy, hard work and time.

She gestures to the old man asleep there in the chair
under the no moon, exhausted by a lifetime of crafting
magical poems that tell the story of the world itself and
the boy understands how serendipity and suffering are
the legs that carry a man to a charmed life. He reaches
through the fence, plucks a peach from the strange tree
and when he twists it open, he finds the key to the museum
hidden where the pit should be and this is what the old man
wakes to see—a boy standing alone, holding a key,
the door of the museum silently swinging open, beckoning.

The Ghost of Karl Ristikivi

In Tartu the rooks are building nests high in the tall trees along
the river. A family of otters plays beneath the bridge.
A fox peers 'round a tree.
     Finally inside the Karl Ristikivi Museum
the old man and the boy settle in for the night. The boy sleeps,
one arm sprawled across a map of the ancient friendly city,
his lips sticky with peaches, but the old man stays up late
typing poems on the computer whose soft blue light laps against
the museum's display cases. Near dawn, the old man looks up,
sensing a presence, smelling smoke.
     He turns to his right and there
is Karl Ristikivi himself, sitting cross-legged in a corner chair
in front of the big bookcases, smoking a cigarette.

The old man is not alarmed and wonders why.
Karl nods and says, "Tere."
The old man says, "Hello Karl, it is an honor to meet you.
Unfortunately, I don't speak Estonian." Karl says, "Don't worry.
I can speak any language I choose now that I am dead."
Outside, the sound of marching boots.
Outside, the rumble of tanks.
Outside, screams and the greedy crackle of fire feeding.

Karl sighs. "I've always traveled. Some things never change.
The sea is a mirror, reflecting the sky. The coast is a harbor.
The end of one way is the beginning of another.
     Nobody remembers tomorrow,
until the day after, when it is gone.
I didn't take anything with me when I fled to Sweden in 1944,
but I return from time to time and where you sit I sat before.

Exile is a long night for the soul."

Silence and the first stain of red brushes the eastern sky.
The old man can hear a sea of harsh voices chanting in turn
Victory for Christ! Für das Vaterland! Za Rodinu!
and then he hears a faltering alto begin to sing
Mu isamaa on minu arm and the chanting fades away.
More and more voices swell with song until surely
the voices of an entire people are singing their love,
their joy and the sun rises and the rooks take wing and whirl
as flowers push through the ashes. The ghost of Karl Ristikivi
leans close and says, "There is always a way out of the labyrinth,
no exile lasts forever." And he is gone.

In the Ruins

Lost four times asking and receiving
directions towards the heart of Tartu
the old man stumbles up a steep hill and
into the remains of an ancient cathedral
built on the bones of a pagan fortress.
Suddenly, he senses what it must be like
to be raised in a thousand year old city
besieged fourteen times conquered raped
pillaged eleven times the oldest forever reinvented
city in the Baltic States where what transpired
600 years ago pulses fresh today.

How well the old man knows what it is
to dwell with the corpse of remorse,
chained to loss, staring at walls
and remembering when this was once
a church, a barn, a water tower,
the sturdy fortress, a library, Daddy's grave
where Mama planted daffodils.
He stands in the tombed cathedral and weeps
while wind rushes through the glassless arches.

What a trickster, Time, speeding faster and faster
until there is time no more, only the hope of rebirth
and a pile of leaning stones' inexorable decline.
For the boy, Time still stretches infinitely each hour
a renaissance, every day a revolution of expectation.
He looks down the hill, awed by the kind bright faces
of the four young people who gave them directions

helped them find their way and he sees clearly
the road they must take from here.
He squeezes the old man's hand reassuringly
and they descend from the ruins
one certain resurrection at a time.

The Ogre's Lunch

The boy stands under the magic tree in the ancient orchard
listening to worms turn in the soil, watching ants quick-march
hither and yon while the old man hangs laundry
on the clothesline behind the museum.
A seagull paces atop the wood shed and two rooks
bob their heads, conversing loudly about the weather.
The boy hasn't realized yet that he
     understands what they are saying.

En appears, out of nowhere, in front of the old man.
They smile hello at each other.
Even though there is every kind of ripe fruit on the magic tree,
it is early April in Nordic Tartu and green is just starting to show
in the grass and buds. A light snow begins to fall
and the rooks rise, clicking and wheezing to themselves.
The old man regrets washing his only pair of long johns.
It will be tomorrow before they dry.

The boy hears a loud metallic rumbling and growling.
It sounds like a grumpy dragon,
     it sounds like the old man sounds
in the early afternoon when he should take a nap but refuses,
saying naps are for babies. The boy looks up from
his nature reverie to see an orange garbage truck
pull up and stop in front of the museum.

Only yesterday, the old man grumbled complaining
there would be no trash pickup at the museum.

The boy watches, astonished, as a beet-faced ogre
        in a filthy jumpsuit
leaps from the back of the truck, opens the gate, hurls aside
a rusted silver washtub the boy hadn't noticed before
        and plucks a small bag out from underneath.

The boy wonders what's in the bag and who put it there.
The ogre stops, turns, menaces the boy with a
furrowed gather of his scraggly eyebrows,
        then walks through the gate,
tossing the bag to the driver of the truck before he
        jumps on the back
and the truck lumbers away panting down the lane.

The old man takes the boy's hand and
        they go for a walk, admiring
the gentle dance of snowflakes and soft
        spring petals through the air.
An hour later, when they return to the museum,
        the boy notices the washtub
has vanished and he hears En laughing from
        somewhere he can't see.
The old man pats the boy on his shoulder.
        "Don't fret, boy," he says,

"I bet En makes lunch for her sons every day and leaves it there
where it will be safe from the rat kings."
        "Oh," says the boy.
"What is a Rat King?" The old man yawns.
        "You know, I think I will take a nap.
Snow in springtime makes me sleepy. Remind me
later and I'll tell you all about the rat kings of Estonia."

What the Old Man Sees Upstairs

As the old man is tucking the boy into bed, the boy looks up
into his eyes and asks, "Do you hear those footsteps upstairs?
I thought we were the only ones staying here in the museum."
The old man says, "Yes, I hear them. I wonder who it is."
It's a cold spring night in Tartu.
The old man and the boy turn toward the window
as a gust of wind whistles through the trees and rain patters
breathy rhythms on the glass. The old man steps to the window
and, squinting, peers out. He sees butterfly shaped snowflakes
fluttering in the rain. He turns back to the boy and says,
"It is time for all good boys to go to sleep."
The boy closes his eyes, yawns, and in minutes
his breathing slows then deepens as he drifts now on clouds.

The old man and the boy have the first floor of the museum
to themselves. The old man has no idea who is upstairs.
He decides to find out. He locates and lights a candle,
opens the door and quietly ascends the staircase.
When he gets to the second floor's door, he leans in and
rests his ear against it, listening for footsteps. He waits waits
waits. No sound. When he leans harder the door opens.
He whispers, "Hello?" No response. Slowly, softly he
pushes the door all the way open. The soft glow of candles
in wall nooks lights the way down a winding corridor.
The old man treads softly with great care to remain silent.
But at the second turn his sleeve catches on the dark sharp
corner of a file cabinet. His sleeve rips loudly.

    He holds still, listening.

No sound. He tiptoes further down the turning passage.
Surely, he has walked for miles now. How can all this
twisting be contained under a single roof? After the fourth turn
he finds himself in a vast room whose domed ceiling
cannot exist under the attic's old rafters and yet it does.
Candles glitter high and low on bookshelves and ivory skulls.
A limestone block carved with flights of swallows,
cornflower bouquets, sits altar-like in the center of the room.
And there is En, crouching in a corner, her lit taper singeing
manuscript pages trembling between her arthritic fingers.
"*Inimene on loodud tööd tegema, lind laulma,*" she says
        and the old man understands her,
understands the book she is burning is the tome of poems
she never wrote, stories she never told because her father said,
"You were born to work, the birds were born to sing," and the
old man gasps and stretches out his hands to stop her even as
pages spark and feather upward and before his eyes transform,
        take wing

and the room is filled with the songs of 339 species of birds—
tits, siskins, loons and grebes, shearwaters and petrels, gannets,
kinglets, waxwings, cormorants, pelicans, bitterns, herons,
egrets, ibis and spoonbills, storks and flamingos, ducks, geese
and swans, osprey and hawks, kites and eagles, grouse,
partridges, cranes and crakes and coots, shrikes and plovers and
magpies and ravens and warblers—

more birds than the old man can name, such a splendor of habit
wing and voice and he thinks of his own father shooting a crow,
how it spiraled down at the edge of the forest and how his father
stepped on the crow so it screamed and cawed for help

how the crow let out such a heart
breaking sound and a vast murder of crows came cawing yet
could not stop the heavy feet of a man tramping on and on
thinking only about duty, how he must lower
the dragline bucket and bring it up again,
great trees dripping from its teeth, drooling rocks and loam

and the boy cried and the wounded crow died but as it died
its spirit lifted to perch on his left shoulder. Decades later,
a lifetime later, and the crow has never left him.
Unfit for work in the world of men, he opens his mouth and
legends creak out, he claws poems from the air
with scaled talons. What a life, to be bird-spirited,
five thousand miles and seventy years from the strip-
mines of his childhood, a Kentucky crow his faithful familiar.
The old man closes his eyes against a wave of loneliness and
when he opens them, he sees he is back in the museum.
Outside, the snow has stopped, a nightjar chirrs peacefully.
The boy dreams he is standing in a blue field of cornflowers,
        swallows dancing the air in every direction,
        the universe a melody begging him to sing, to sing,
        to never stop singing.

The Wolf at the Door

Candlelight, starlight, the wolf is at the door.
The old man and the boy sit on a curb in Tartu
surrounded by the old man's books. The boy
has put their last Euros in an upturned hat and
jangles them hopefully at each passerby while
the old man holds a piece of cardboard on which
he has written, "The Voice of Authenticity: only €5."

Once upon a time, when a bard was the feasted guest
and children went berrying while women sought
mushrooms in the cool forest's litter, wolves watched
waiting in the oaky shadows, hungering for a bite
of Mats and Madis, Epp or Piret. Guns and drums
taught wolves caution but if you are hungry you will
gnaw a man to his bones and eat his drum skin too.

These days, wolves are not as plentiful as poets
but they eat better than artists ever do as folks find
happiness in office blocks and streaming cellphones
and the woods grow rich again with rabbits grazing.
Earlier this year, a gray wolf fell into the Pärnu River.
The construction foreman yelled, "Save him!" and
three brave men dove into the crashing icy torrent.

What has the world come to when a wolf stud rides
wrapped in a pink blanket to the vet's office while
meaty hands pat his head and voices murmur,
"Good dog, good dog." The bard falls asleep in the gutter

remembering how it should be. He begins to snore.
A long muzzle pokes 'round a signpost, twin yellow eyes
blink slowly, beaconing, and the boy rises and softly
follows the wolf into the woods of Tartu to hunt rabbits.

The Monsters

The old man cannot write any more today. The sky has been
fretting storms for hours, and his knees and back solemnly
opine spring will never take root in Estonia's snow and rain.

The boy is half-hidden behind a tent-flap of tablecloth
in a fortress he's made of the round table in the corner,
clutching a book of Estonian folktales, saucer-wide eyes

racing across the page. The book's cover shines with gilt
figures of gnomes and mermaids, strange shapes shifting
from one form to another. The old man remembers how he

loved mythology as a child, could name every creature,
each deity rumored to dwell in mountain, cave and sea.
A peculiar feeling wells up inside the old man. He wonders

whose monster is he? There are consequences one faces
living to be seventy, and he has never walked carefully,
confident every step he took was along the hero's path,

his every action a bold right action. How startled he was
the first time someone looked at him with fear and revulsion,
then how angry—why couldn't they see
         the good heart beaming

beneath his freakish exterior, sense that he wished them the
joy, wonder and excitement he felt wandering the mysteries
the world offers, eager to explore, life one terrific adventure?

Age has shown him how small kindnesses mist away while
memory seizes and carves deep each terror and harm, every
hurt feeling and slight. Somewhere, someone still nurses scars

and tells an awful tale of how his path slashed across theirs.
Who is writing the book of his life?
    The old man squints at the boy
suddenly suspicious and the boy looks up from his reading,

his young face radiant and trusting. "Did you know,"
    the boy confides,
"there are more than forty words for witch in Estonian
    and as many
wise and good conjurers as wicked ones?
    I wonder how you can tell

which witch is which?" He giggles and the old man smiles.
    "I bet En's a witch," the boy says,
    "and monsters really live in Estonia."
"I bet you're right," the old man says,
    "I bet if we look hard enough

we can see them everywhere."

When Everything Blossoms

The old man sits under the Brazilian orchid tree
in the tropical greenhouse at the Tartu botanical gardens.
After a week of April snow, it feels good to be warm.
He once knew a woman obsessed with plants, her yards
filled with flowers, fruiting trees, window sills crammed
with pots of orchids. When the lawns were full, she
planted the easements and hellstrips. Flower seeds
drifted down to root in the sidewalks surrounding her house,
even potholes in the street bloomed during years the wind
blew right. For decades, he has tried to forget her but now
how he wishes she were here to witness this marvel:
10,000 species gathered from tundra and rainforest,
woodland, field, and meadow all blossoming at once.
He remembers her ivory skin, her unruly hair, the sweet
full curve of her lower lip. He takes a postcard from his
coat pocket and in his cramped cursive writes:

My beloved my beloved oh how
I miss you in every season
my heart cries out for you
I can do without food and water
I can do without sun and moon
I can do without the stars in the night sky
but oh my love what misery to live without you

The boy is dancing through the hothouse jungle, resisting
the temptation to swing from cascading liana vines, his feet
just missing false bird-of-paradise, the fireworks bloom

of bromeliads. The old man fills the card, turns it,
crosshatches more lines the other way.
What white van, boxcar or plane can carry
the great weight of longing he feels for her?
He imagines his postcard curling in the cavernous
hold of a sturdy ocean-going vessel steaming across
the cold gray Atlantic, ink bleeding and blurring.

After all this time he can't quite remember her address.
He affixes three pink stamps to the tiny card and writes
her name and "the tan house with a green roof near
the Ohio River where daffodils, tulips and hyacinths
edge the tumbledown fence, where a lilac bush shelters
sweet lily-of-the-valley and sprays of bleeding hearts."
What are the chances it will reach her? How do
African cactus and bougainvillea from Brazil flower
in the same Estonian bed? When no one is looking,
the old man plucks a red begonia bud, tucks its waxy
shimmer in his buttonhole. He calls to the boy,
"Let's find a mailbox!" and off they go, into the narrow
cobbled streets of Tartu where it is spring and
the world is fresh and burgeoning.

Midnight on Toome Hill

A Seto woman and, by the look of her, a gypsy. He instantly
knows she is a witch. The old man sees her clearly under
the starry moonlight, just after midnight, as he crosses the
top of Toome Hill, on his long walk back to the Karl Ristikivi

Museum, 18 K.A. Hermanni, his writer residence. He has
seen this woman before but can't recall where. Wrapped in
scarves, she huddles by her bright fire. She is burning bones.
Four linen bags, stitched with animal shapes and runed

symbols, spilling bones, are placed at each corner of the fire.
The old man had heard her voice when he neared the top of
the hill. She is singing now, a wind woven guttural shamanic
sound summoning who knows what from spirit realms. He

draws closer to the woman and her fire. Mesmerized, he sits,
quietly, watching and listening. Suddenly the woman stops
singing, turns and stares direct and deep into his eyes. In an
instant he is transported to a pew in the little country Southern

Baptist church he grew up in. A hellfire and brimstone
evangelist, visiting for the annual summer revival, is jumping
up and down, barely catching his breath, rhythmically shouting
a sermon full of the wrath of God, of lightning and rolling
    thunder,

of fiery furnaces, of eternal spiritual punishment for material
misdeeds, of the slaughter of kings, of the destruction and

annihilation of kingdoms when, in the middle of the
    Old Testament sermon,
the boy watches as his old, frail Aunt Sis stands up from

the fourth row, down front to the right where she always
sits, and with her eyes closed she says "Jesus Christ gave us the
eight Beatitudes in his Sermon on The Mount." The evangelist
stops preaching and stares fiercely at her, but she doesn't see

him because her eyes are closed. She recites,
Blessed are the poor in spirit, for theirs is the kingdom of heaven.
    Blessed are they who mourn, for they shall be comforted.
    Blessed are the meek, for they shall inherit the earth.
    Blessed are they who hunger and thirst for righteousness,
    for they shall be satisfied. Blessed are the merciful, for they
    shall obtain mercy. Blessed are the pure of heart, for they
    shall see God. Blessed are the peacemakers, for they shall be
    called children of God. Blessed are they who are persecuted
    for the sake of righteousness, for theirs is the kingdom of
    heaven.

The old man doesn't speak. He listens and watches as
the Seto woman takes more bones from her four bags and
places them in the fire. In a deep resonating voice
the woman calls out words the old man doesn't understand.

Yellow eyes appear through the branches. The she-wolf howls,
a howl that quakes from the beginning to the ending of time.
The wolf looks into the old man and the Seto woman. Now
the old man hears the voice of William Blake,

*The roaring of lions, the howling of wolves, the raging of the
  stormy sea, and the destructive sword, are portions of
  eternity too great for the eye of man.*

Without opening her jaws, the she-wolf speaks,
"Welcome, old man. Welcome to Toome Hill.
I will be here for you if you need me." Then she is gone.

The boy wakes the old man. It is well past sunrise.
The boy says, "There will be celebrations at the National
Museum today. Let's go." The old man yawns, softly smiles
and says to the boy,

> "My dreams have been quite odd since arriving
> here in Tartu. Give me a minute and I'll be ready.
> I'll tell you all about my strange dream on the way."

Words Worth Dying For

Some words are worth dying for, some better left unsaid.
Nods across the street, a friendly hello to the checkout clerk,
rambling chat about the weather with a stranger, these things
are rare in Estonia. The old man has roamed around the world
      parlaying the gentle neighborliness he learned as a
      Kentucky farm boy into rich friendships everywhere.
Yet here, in what his elementary school maps called the Soviet
      Union—one tremendous red sweep of strangeness and
      threat—which now for a long generation has breathed
      independence as Eesti,
small talk is dead.

The hammer and sickle cut deep in the year before his birth
sweeping nearly 21,000 souls into cattle cars rattling to Siberia,
ten thousand and more women, six thousand and more babes
and children torn from their fields and meadows, their ancient
war-ravaged cities to die or to survive far from their homes.
And for those left behind?

The forced public bow to the system, tension, trepidation,
each word weighed to avoid betraying friend or family to the
occupying fate. How many more were seized for prison camps,
left to rot in insane asylums? Such omnipresent foreboding
the worst thing—you might speak a word that doomed
another. Better surely to say nothing at all, sit alone
when you can, exchange guarded glances with one who might
think as you do until the spirit of the times cries, "Rise! Act!"

While the boy tours the thirteen prison cells,
three dark interrogation chambers of the KGB dungeons
in that purposefully innocuous gray building with metal bars
across the cellar windows, the old man goes to Werner Café
and sits by himself. He is tired; he doesn't want to see the
metal bunk beds with their striped stained mattresses,
the low-ceilinged long corridors, a restraining chair where
words refused to spill forth in tortured gasps.

He is tired and full of grief. In his homeland, the two-minute
hate is boiling again, this hour calls for a wall, the next
brings diatribes against the poor, the browns and blacks,
the queers, Muslims, Jews, the educated. He sits in Estonia
writing a poem about the ouroboros of kleptocracy,
a totalitarian serpent circling the world, its destructive jaws
centered now over Austria, now nearing Italy,
now churning America, now gyring Greece and Poland,
summoning zealots and mavericks of every persuasion,
spewing xenophobia, nationalism, populism, nepotism and
        autocracy,
shitting out edicts and bans, moratoriums, executive orders
all stamped "For the Good of the People" by parliaments,
congresses, oligarchies, juntas, senates and judiciaries.

Rise up! he writes. *Don't bow down! Now is the time to act!*
Fight back against, sing and dance and write against social,
political and cultural control reined to the will of corrupt and
charismatic despots who begin by mocking and neutering
the press, insidiously imposing censorship, propaganda,
indoctrination of the young in schools of no-thought,
emboldening and funding an ever-more-militarized police force,
uniting the country in a rhetoric of revulsion toward the other,

the stranger, the one whose skin, whose religion, whose culture,
whose sex, whose language is fuel for the hideous ecstasy of
hatred and fear. And what purpose does the purposeful stirring
of fear and hatred serve? Distraction!

Distraction from the crimes of the government,
distraction as a fattening few hoard power, hide wealth,
distraction as corporations ruin the earth herself
to feed insatiable greed. Refuse! Refuse to be distracted,
oh my brothers, oh my sisters, oh my daughters, oh my sons!
See the serpent for what it is, the hypocritical mask of
charlatans and hucksters whose only care for you
is concern that you will continue to serve them;
know in your hearts that no atrocity, no lie, no genocide,
no abomination is beyond them if they can profit from it.

In a country where small talk is dead yet behemoths were cast
out by ordinary folk singing songs, recrafting tales,
     writing poems,
the old man looks into the eyes of passersby, silently promising
to spend his remaining words wisely, and he writes and writes.

Taking Out the Trash

The old man skulks about town after dark
    like a nocturnal squirrel looking for places
    to ditch his small bags of trash.
As he walks, he thinks about the squirrels in his head,
    their secretive ways, the amazing unpleasant things
    they've stashed for years and unearth at unexpected
    moments, the monologues they hold about the broken
    crap in his mind: "Should we keep this?
    Will this come in handy sometime?
    Shall we chew on this a while?"
Whenever he stops focusing on keeping them at bay,
the squirrels in his head sneak in more junk he doesn't want,
and some days all his energy is spent trying to maintain
the semblance of mental hygiene, a vaguely well-ordered brain.

The old man's trash bursts all over the street
    as he's trying to cram it into the small-holed receptacle
    outside the information center.
It's not high tourist season in Tartu but heads swivel
    as the bag gives way and spills coffee grounds, empty vials
    of herbs the woman who loved plants once filled so he
    can maintain the fine balance of his nerves,
    crumpled cookie bags.
The old man loves cookies; they console him,
    remind him of his mother, a woman who understood
    without needing to be told what it meant
to be born high-strung and spirited in a town of 323 souls and
discover you've got wanderlust in a place that treasures roots.

The boy is tired of sneaking about; he says,
    "Sheesh. How do you manage to generate so much trash?
    Every day, we have to find a new spot to dump it.
    No one else seems to be carrying around bags of garbage;
    you should burn it in the barrel out back by the
    woodshed? That's what I'd do."

"Wait till you grow up," the old man says.
    "You'll be surprised how your life changes."
Secretly, he's ashamed and also worried about what neighbors
        would think if they saw how much he throws away.
It's true he has yet to see anyone else unfurling plastic bags of
        refuse from backpacks to bins along the avenues.
And how can he tell if anyone else carries a complement of
        jabbering squirrels in their heads, squirrels
clutching at perfect nonsense, constantly chattering,
        chiding, criticizing or keening sharp alarm
        every time he thinks for himself?
He wonders about this as he walks on.
        He never mentions the squirrels to anyone,
they are worse than having a mad grandmother
        who sets herself on fire,
far worse than walking in on your second wife
        entertaining in the nude.
He decides yes, every grown person
        likely has squirrels or monkeys, hedgehogs or rabbits
        peeking out through their eyes and if that's true,
they understand these unwelcome familiars must be dealt with
every day lest they overrun the brain with their rubbish.

His attitude shifts. No more skulking,
        he says to himself, just get rid of what you need to every

day, as best you can, and if you're seen...so what?
Maybe your predicament will make someone else smile,
remind them they're not the only ones with troubles.
The boy points; there's a dumpster down the street.
"I think we've hit the jackpot!" he says
and the old man answers querulously, "That *might* be
big enough," and then they are laughing and all is well again.

The Language of Angels

At least once or twice or three times every day
the old man and the boy
walk the two kilometers downtown,
    from the Karl Ristikivi Museum,
their home for a few weeks during the old man's
    Tartu Writer Residency.

The old man loves to see all the children and young people
      walking and running and bicycling
      up and down the wide paths next to the roads and
      through the parks.
Estonia has only been a free and independent country

for twenty eight years. He sees and feels
    youthful spirit everywhere. It fills the air.
At the crosswalk a car slows then stops.
    The old man is astonished;
    pedestrians really do have the right of way
    here in Estonia.

Walkers, runners, and bikers don't even pause,
    they keep right on moving
    while the car or truck comes to a complete stop.
The old man takes the boy's hand and they walk quickly
    across the street. They take their time

climbing and crossing Toome Hill, then descending
     under Angel's Bridge, down the winding cobbled streets
     of old Tartu to the 13th Century St. John's Cathedral.
The old man has always liked old churches and

graveyards. They take a seat on the seventh row.
     The priest stands and reads a passage
     from the back of the Bible, in Estonian.
Although the old man doesn't understand a word
     of what is being read,
     he knows his Bible,

and with the book open to the end it must be from
     the Book of Revelation. He wonders what passage
     it could possibly be. Then he hears a voice say
And he showed me a pure river of water of life, clear as

crystal, proceeding out of the throne of God.
A master begins to play the old baroque organ. Sacred music
     resounds throughout the holy cathedral,
     lifting the old man's spirits.
Since he was in his Mama's belly

he's listened to and loved music, all kinds of music.
     He especially loves spiritual music, in its myriad shapes
     and forms. He was born
     into a musical Kentucky family.
His mother, the oldest of thirteen, sang alto, and, like her

father, his grandfather, she could play any instrument
     she picked up. The old man has always loved
     the music of nature and nature includes human beings.

He feels and believes music is the language of angels,

a gift to humans. As the organ sounds one final glorious song,
the old man is lifted up out of his pew, through the air,
up to and through the ceiling,
into the arms of angels.

On the Terrible Loneliness of Heroes

The old man wakes from dreaming the beginning of the world:
a bird lifts from a briary nest and her three eggs hatch. The
golden egg cracks open to reveal the sun, the silver egg
parts under the sharp edge of a crescent moon erupting,
the mottled blue and green egg discloses the earth. The boy
has been up since dawn, puzzling over the book of myths.

In his imagination, the boy is a great and crafty hero standing
by the edge of the Baltic Sea waiting for the White Ship
to take him away to the place of new beginnings. The Old
Empty One lurks nearby in the shadows, wearing a Hat of
Fingernails that makes him invisible, though no less ogrish
or stupid. The boy can smell him there and knows he
will outwit the devil yet again. The world is shifting.

Forests are upping root and travelling on; they are done with
cruel greedy people who hardened their hearts against nature.
The boy wears a red belt woven with protection spells
pulled tight against his slender waist.
    "I am a hero," he says aloud, "I am the hero!"
The old man holds his breath, his white beard sparkling
against the thin pillow, wondering if now is a good time
to tell the boy how it is to live as a hero.

Legends are lonely all their lives, he muses.
        Heroes are never invited to go bowling, for a long
        weekend's island camping trip, or to Easter dinner.
        No one asks a hero if he wants to see the latest action film.

Surely the hero has better things to do and wouldn't enjoy
        singing 'round the fire while marshmallows brown;
        certainly he'd laugh at Hollywood's anemic
        simulation of mighty deeds!
A hero should be off unearthing sacred stones,
        returning stolen magic pipes to the Lightning God
        so farmers might have rain again, retrieving a sword
        from the depths of a stream where a scheming wizard
        has trapped it.

Ah, and love!

The boy doesn't understand romantic love yet, cannot know
how heroes never enjoy small domestic blisses, there are no
evening strolls in the garden to see if the carrots have sprouted.
It's always love-'em-&-leave-'em, occasionally enlivened by an
adrenaline pumping rescue, then a swift farewell to a chorus of
"We will never forget you!" as destiny races you on. How can
this hold a candle to the joy of learning another's body—
discovering how it pulses, thrills and stirs—
over the course of decades? It cannot.

And twenty years after you're dead—
        munched by a monster, poisoned by a demon,
        accidentally cutting off your leg with a bewitched sword,
        forgetting the way out of the bog, falling in love
        with a water nymph, tumbled by your medals
        into the sea—there is every chance
modern youngsters will refuse to believe anyone would
ever do all the crazed holy-fool things you did; it must be some
bullshit the old folks dreamed up to keep children in line,
another story with a useful moral hidden in there somewhere.

O, child, the old man longs to say, it's a damned lonely life, it's dangerous and you'll be misunderstood and people will tell more lies than truth about you even when you're right there, listening. Instead he says, "Good morning, Son of the Sun! Shall we have eggs for breakfast? We must fortify ourselves for another day adventuring!" And while they fix their meal, he tells the boy the story of three eggs hatching the universe, he adds a fourth egg for the stars, a fifth for the rainbow. Time enough for the boy to discover how lonely it is to live as a legend. Let everything be magic for him now while the old man guards the never-ending secret loneliness of heroes.

The Kentucky Lion

The old man and the boy are late for the meeting at the Tartu
Literature House. They had stopped on Toome Hill
    to watch young
couples dancing to music wafting from an unseen source. By

the time they finally arrive, the meeting is adjourning.
Marja Unt opens doors to an adjacent room and the party
begins. The old man wonders if he has been invited

because he looks strange to Estonians with his long hair,
    braided, sewn and stitched beard,
and the dragon tattoo on his cheek. What in the world
will the response to him be? Friendly, he hopes. He never

knows what to expect in situations like this.
    He decided a long time ago
that, regardless of where he was or who he was with, he would
simply be himself, a friendly Kentucky farm boy.
    He is introduced to

Arne Merilai, Head of the University of Tartu's
    Estonian Literature
Department, and they exchange names. Arne proclaims,
"Ah! The Kentucky Lion!"
    The old man looks at him, bewildered,

wondering where that came from.
    Being called The Kentucky Lion,

out of the blue, in Tartu, throws him for a loop.
	Arne says, "Oskar Luts,
one of our great writers, wrote *Kevade, Spring,* one of the most

popular books in Estonian literature. In it, the mischievous
character Joosep Toots loves Native Americans and dreams
of running away to America some day. Toots called himself

The Kentucky Lion. You remind me of Toots! Toots's stories
and language had a great impact on our language and culture."
The old man says, "Thank you." After more pleasant

introductions and conversations, he and the boy cry "Goodbye!
Goodbye!" and wander through the click clackety
	cobbled streets,
heading back to the museum.

The old man considers what it means to be a lion,
a fearless leader free to roam, or trapped and enslaved,
	ceaselessly pacing back and forth inside a cage.
In his long life he has experienced both.
	He has always felt that his natural position

as a poet, never craving the world's esteem, is to fight for
freedom, equality, and justice for all people, for all people.
He really doesn't care what people call him.
	He's been called every name in the book,

some good, some terrible. Atop Toome Hill they pause
where the young couples had danced, and,
		hand in hand, stare up to the bright stars
		the near full moon. The boy says, "This place is magic."

The old man, straightening his back and shoulders and proudly
raising his head yet further toward the night sky, lets out a
deep loud roar, then turns and looks at the boy. The boy, eyes

bulging, astonished, says, "Wow! You really are a lion!"
Then the boy lets out a loud squeaky growl.
    They laugh and as one prowl
down the hill into the starlit Tartu night.

The Angel's Bridge

En told them they should hold their breath while crossing
Angel's Bridge in Tartu and so they do. The boy fervently
believes that doing this will make his dearest wish come true
because En said it would, yet as soon as he swells his lungs
and steps onto the cheerful yellow bridge built 181 years ago,
he imagines he is a whale streaking silently through the ocean
as playful dolphins tickle his sides, trying to get him to jump
up into the sweet blue air above and breathe, so he changes
imaginings. Now he is an otter slicking swiftly through a river,
able to go eight long minutes underwater and he can feel the
bushy bristle of the otter's whiskers and this is how, crossing
the Angel's Bridge, he wishes for a huge fan of whiskers,
a wish that will certainly one day come true.

The old man has scoured his high school Latin to puzzle out
the phrase carved on the side of the bridge. He thinks it means
"Rest restores strength." He wonders if the slow weakening of
his joints with each passing year is tied to his aging brain's
tantruming refusal to sleep through the night. Restless, he
writes postcard after postcard to the woman who loves flowers
and every day, he peers through the three finger holes of the
dark cracked wooden mailbox affixed to the pink plaster wall
of the Karl Ristikivi Muuseum to see if there might be anything
inside for him. He knows this is ridiculous, none of his cards
have room for a return address, how could she write back?

Yet he cannot help but hope.
        Today, there was a piece of paper inside. His heart

pirouetted, his fingers trembled as they undid
the broken clothespin and the mailbox door gaped open.
It was an ad for pizza.
He went back inside the museum.
"Come on, kid, let's get a slice!"

All the way to the bridge, the boy has been looking for turtles.
He picks up each round flat stone he finds and carefully
turns it over to make sure it's not a baby turtle.
The old man doesn't have the heart to tell him there are no
native turtles in Estonia, just a pet slider named Fernando
who made the news last year by managing to survive
three years lost on his own. The old man thinks about walking
through the woods with the woman who loves flowers, how she
examined every log for lizards, how she'd point to the great
blue herons on the riverbank and stand on one leg as they did
and say "That's **my** bird," how she discovered a tree whose base
was rotted hollowly away yet one long limb still bloomed
pink and budded green along one and she crowed,
"That tree is **ME**!" She was the breath of spring that gusted

life into his worn wintered heart and without her,
his sap does not rise. He heard a story once about a man
who rushed to the hospital to hold the hand of his high-school
sweetheart as she lay dying. "You were the love of my life,"
he whispered, words he'd felt since the day they met
but had never spoken aloud to her. They had lived their lives
apart, he siring children, cradling grandchildren and great-
grandchildren, she numbing herself in bottle after bottle of
red wine. She opened her faded blue eyes and looked into his.
"Thank you," she said, "you were the love of my life,"
and in their exchange of seven small words, they worked

a tremendous accepting forgiving incantation that mended
every hurt wrong thing between them as she sighed her last.
What would the old man say if he could see his darling again?

He steps onto the bridge. The boy is nearly to the other side.
The old man breathes in. The air he inhales is a canticle of
tree pollen, flower nectar, a sexy heady mix singing life
deep into every secret crevasse, each dendritic branch
of his lungs. He makes his wish, his wish to return
to a springtime of the soul, his heartfelt desire
for another chance with her, and as he begins to walk across
he feels strength surging in his muscles, listens to his tendons
and knees relax, restore, and he knows he can hold his breath
for as long it takes—however long it takes—
to make it to where she waits for him on the other side.

The Illusion of Choice

The machine in the lobby of the ancient government
building has 16 buttons, eight on each side. You can
choose whatever delicious drink you want!

The old man puts in a euro, presses a button marked
espresso. Gear grind, the machine whirrs and spits into
a tiny plastic cup. The boy adds a round of coins, pushes

"Lemon Tea." Again, the endless grinding of gears,
grumbling, loud long spitting, whirring. A second cup
creeps forth from the belly of the machine.

The boy and the old man raise their cups. "Terviseks,"
they say as they touch cups and drink. They screw
up their faces simultaneously, whatever is in here

has more in common with urn cleaner than coffee
or tea. They trade cups, take another sip each.
Whatever is in their cups is exactly the same thing.

"The buttons were a lie!" the boy says. "This is how
it is all over the world," the old man proclaims.
"You step up to the machine and make a choice.

The government asks you for your money and
promises you exactly what you need in exchange.
You wait for a long time, listen to the machine

sputter on and on, and then it serves up the same
unpalatable shit for everyone, whatever it feels like
giving you. Drink up and enjoy your civics lesson.

Terviseks!"

The Old Man Is Kicked Out of Church

On the morning before Easter the old man and the boy
take a pilgrimage by bus to Tallinn. It has been years since
the old man has visited the magical city of domed cathedrals.

The old man and the woman who loves flowers had once,
hand in hand, explored the cobbled streets and alleys. He
looks down at the boy. Even though the old man has been

stumbling a little more often than usual, and holding onto
doorways when he makes a turn, in so many ways he still
feels like a boy himself. He turns his gaze out the window

and watches the Estonian countryside racing by. He is old
now. With his chronic heart disease, every morning when
he wakes up he says, "Thank you for this new day, and

for this adventure my life has been and continues
miraculously to be." So on this gorgeous April
day-before-Easter Saturday morning, as the sun rises

over Estonia, as the bus arrives in Tallinn the old man
whispers "Thank you" to his body for the amazing ride
it's still taking him on. The old man was raised Southern

Baptist. Being forever curious, living in a perpetual state
of wonder at the world and its spellbindingly beautiful and
horrifyingly terrible mysteries, he soon went his own way.

.

At an early age he decided that the fascinating stories of
religion, his own and others', were ways for folks to express
and understand, as much as possible, what is unknowable,

yet often, at least for some, experienceable. He has had so
many near death experiences and visits with spirits. Since
boyhood he has studied the world's religions and spiritualities,

belief and non-belief philosophies, folktales, myths, stories
of alchemy, magic, shamanism, the unknown, close encounters
of every kind. In the early afternoon the old man and the boy

enter the gigantic Eastern Orthodox church, at the top of
Parliament Hill. It is packed with pilgrims come to pray and
pay homage to Jesus, getting ready to celebrate Easter.

The old man and the boy are mesmerized by the gold
ornamentation, the gorgeous art and sculpture filling the
cathedral. A group has gathered toward the front, to the

left, chanting, praying, singing. The smell of beeswax candles
and incense fills the air. Someone taps on the old man's
shoulder. He turns. A young man asks, in English, "Are you

Orthodox?" all the while staring at the dragon tattoo on the
old man's cheek. The old man, startled out of spiritual reverie,
blurts, "No." The young official says, "This is only for the

Orthodox." The old man, embarrassed, says, "I'm so sorry.
I am deeply spiritual. I am honoring, paying respects. Thank
you, we will leave." The young man nods. The old man grabs

the boy's hand and they head out the door. The boy asks, "What happened? Why were we asked to leave the church? What did we do wrong?" The old man, upset that he was just

kicked out, wondering what Jesus would think of the lavishly ornamented cathedral, says, "Nothing, It was a mistake. Everything is fine. Let's find the old wall and wander for a

while." As they stumble down the ancient alleys, the cobbled streets, as the boy marvels at signs and sculptures of owls and roosters, and dragons and wolves, the old man

reviews his life. Why is he here, in this world, in this life? His first goal in life has been to find the missing pieces. Where were they? Where was God? He has always wanted to

stare deep into the eyes of God, to know God, to be one with God. Whatever that means. He realizes that the gift of poetry, sung and unsung, has time and again proven to be

the most trusted way for him to honestly and openly express his deepest emotions, his intimately personal experiences, what he values more than all else, what moves deep in his

soul. He learned to listen, with his heart, with his intuition. What else can he possibly do? When the old man looks up from his walking waking dream, he sees a sign. At first, he

wonders if it's for a magic theater, but then he realizes it is some strange church. He and the boy step closer. It is a small church. The wooden door is beautifully painted.

The old man can see now that this is the
       Ukrainian Greek-Catholic
Church of the Mother of God with Three Hands. The what?
Now he wants to know more so he and the boy enter. The

first thing they see is a spiritually inspired primitive painting of
St. Hildegard of Bingen, that visionary writer, mystic
and natural scientist. If the boy had a patron saint it would be

St. Hildegard of Bingen. A friendly man steps forward and
introduces himself. He says he helped the local parish build
the church. He is a joy to talk with. He invites the old man and

the boy back in the morning for the Easter Sunday service.
The old man says, "We'll be here." The next morning they
return. The boy brings a small bouquet of flowers. It is a

holy ghost service. After the long beautiful opening prayers,
the red-robed priest retires behind the iconostasis and
re-emerges in a beautiful spring-flower embroidered set of

white robes. With a joyful smile, he invites everyone to
troop outside the church. Then the priest stands by the
painted door as prayers are sung, bells jangle, incense

burns. The old man can feel what is happening even
though he doesn't understand a word. The priest hammers
on the closed doors to the church three times with the base

of a cross and the doors are opened. The old man knows
that as everyone stood outside, the Spirit had worked miracles,
likely transubstantiation of the bread and wine into the body

and blood, and the congregation is now going inside to receive
communion. The old man and the boy do not go with them.
The old man feels a sense of wonder he knows will stay

with him for the rest of his life. As they walk away from the
Easter Sunday service, down the lost alley, the old man says,
"Now I will call that The Magic Theater of Tallinn." The boy

asks, "Is it true? The stories, the myths, the religions, the
Easter service. Are Jesus and God real?" Looking up beyond
the parapets, the old man replies, "Yes, dear boy, the folktales,

the legends, the myths, the religions, Jesus, God, all of it is
poetry, every word of it is the truth." The boy says, "I believe it.
All of it. Now let's get something to eat. I'm starving."

The Field Guide

He sees her where she cannot be; today in a 1952 Swedish
field guide to birds with carefully penciled Estonian
superscriptions buried in the bookstore's bargain
bin. The old man stands in the sturdy ancient
walled shadows and traces illustrated sparrows,
wrens and buntings with his wrinkled fingertips. He
remembers how she fed the birds each morning, hanging
lumps of homemade suet in netted onion bags from
the plum tree's branches. When they walked
together, all those years ago, she'd claim
each fallen feather from the ground, admire it and
stick it in his hatband. He was entranced with her delight.
She knew the name of every bird; she said them as
tenderly as she said his name. Sometimes they'd
cut through an alley and he'd see his shadow
striding ahead of them, his hat throwing feather
shadows in every direction, hair wind-lifting, and
he'd think to himself: "If my heart grows any happier,
it will take wing, it will leave me." This is exactly
what happened; he flew away from her yet
his body never forgot its habit of happiness.
He turns a new leaf and a feather falls from between
two pages of watercolor falcons. He creaks over to pick
it up, tucks it in his lapel. She was his field guide to joy;
the lessons she blithely offered ones he cannot unlearn.

The Magic of Rejection

The old man walks outside to find the boy perched on a log
by the mailbox in front of the museum. Last week, the boy
wrote his very first poem and sent it off to the oldest literary
magazine in Estonia. It is the best poem ever; the boy is
sure it will be accepted. The first three days after he mails it,
the boy chants the poem to himself, savoring each syllable.
The fourth day, he begins to check the mailbox.
Today, he woke to the cascading song of finches and knew
this would be the day he received good news from *Looming*.

The boy's not entirely certain how major magazines go about
accepting poems and he doesn't want to ask the old man.
He hasn't told the old man about the poem; the old man writes
poetry, endless hours a day muttering lines to himself, and the
boy's a little worried that the old man would tell him how this
or that might be better. The boy knows his poem is perfect;
he doesn't want to change a thing even to please his friend.

He thinks he knows how the news will come. A beautiful
woman in scarlet livery sparkling with brass buttons will stride
down K. A. Hermanni bearing a carved mahogany box. She will
smile—the most beatific smile!—and when he takes the box,
she will bow and hand him a golden key. The boy can feel how
easily the key will snick the lock open. Inside, he'll see a folded
parchment bound in blue silk ribbon. He can hear the ribbon's
whisper as he unties it, the animal rustle of vellum unfolding.
The margins of the note are brilliant with vermillion flourishes
and the calligraphic text reads simply, "Yes! Yes! Yes!"

The boy yelps with pleasure; the beautiful woman applauds.

But as the old man steps outside, he sees the boy's shoulders
shaking with anger, shame and sorrow and the boy is sobbing,
cradling his face in both hands. A torn envelope, a crumpled
piece of paper are at his feet. "Dear boy!" the old man exclaims,
"what is wrong? Are you hurt? Show me where!" The boy lifts
his snot-streaked face and howls, "They didn't want my poem!
I am a failure!" The old man picks up the paper, unwads it.
It's a faded mimeograph, not even a full page, just a slip with
no salutation and no signature. It reads,
>"Not right for us. Sorry.
>You might try again. Good luck."

The old man says, "Scoot over," and he sits beside the boy
while the boy cries and cries. "How can they be so cruel?"
the boy wails. "They didn't say even one nice thing!"
The old man smooths the rejection slip. "Boy, you've told me
many secrets so I'll tell you one in turn. This paper is magic."

The boy looks at him in utter disbelief but before he can open
his mouth to argue, the old man continues, "Here's how it is.
Rejection is magic for those who allow it to work its magic.
We are all drawn to create; we are the species that paints and
sings, draws and writes, dances, sculpts, makes photographs.
We are born to it; it is our earliest urge. But we are also fearful,
worried what others think of us and so—for most—a single no
is the end of it. No more poems, no more beauty given freely
to the world without a second thought.
>But you are not like that."

"I am different?" the boy asks. "Oh, yes," the old man says,
and puts his arm around the boy's shoulder. "You are different.

I know you can see great magic hidden in this piece of paper.
I bet you'll frame it and put it on the wall above your desk,
wherever your desk is in the world. You will look at it when
you sit down to write. You will say to yourself,
> 'The worst has happened—I banished all fear of rejection
> when I was brave enough to risk and survive it.
> All that matters to me is creating.'

One day, you find this soulless no has changed and has become
the sound of your words ringing everywhere because you never
stopped believing in the gift you were given, you never
grew shy about sharing it, either. Do you understand?'"

"Yes, yes, yes!" the boy exclaims. "May I run down to the
secondhand store to see if there's a lovely frame there,
maybe a fancy one in mahogany with some pretty carving?"
Before the old man can answer, before he can say yes or no,
the boy has dashed down K.A. Hermanni, shouting his poem
to strangers as he speeds by. A pretty woman smiles.
"What a beautiful poem," she says as he passes her on the
narrow lane, but the boy can only think of this poem, and the
next poem waiting to be written, and the one after that, and
he doesn't even see her, he never hears her praise.

In the Cathedral of Crows

There are 101 churches in Estonia, cathedrals
looming on hills, tiny chapels tucked in valleys,
everywhere kirk and temple doors thrown open

desperately beckoning as the truly holy gasps
under the relentless press of entertainment and
a quick buck. The old man is sick of churches.

At sunset, he is ambling the banks of the
Emajõgi River when the cawing of a thousand
crows startles him from his walking trance.

In his daydream, the woman who loves flowers is
seated at the prow of a broad-beamed barge,
drifting toward him with the tide. In her left hand

she holds a bouquet of rook feathers, in her right hand
a nest full of crow eggs. The old man, coming back to
himself, realizes the boy has disappeared. He turns

quickly, scanning left and right, before, behind, then
with rising panic, the weedy river and its brown water.
Can the boy even swim? He doesn't know; he could

not when he was a boy himself. The boy is nowhere.
The old man looks up into the tall trees. There are
crows everywhere: on nests, on branches, in the air

circling, swoop-diving, ascending. He's never seen
so many crows. "I bet they've been nesting here for

centuries," he mutters. He sees the boy then,

hands clasped as if in prayer, kneeling on the grass
in the center of a broad avenue of beech, looking up
awestruck as the great host rises and settles above.

The branches of the trees arch and meet, the red
and gold and orange and pink sunset streaming light
finer than stained glass, sacred nature's cathedral.

A rook feather drifts down from one of the hundred
nests above; the old man reaches out and catches it
before it hits the ground. He slips it into his shirt pocket,

next to his heart. Beside the boy, he spots half of a
jagged-edged spotted crow egg in among the belled
blue wildflowers. He picks it up and cups it in his hands.

The rooks rise once more as bells toll the last tones of
vespers and the sun slips away. With deep reverence,
he kneels beside the boy and they bow their heads

together in the cathedral of crows, their every breath
a prayer.

Homeland

How to tell the smiling Estonian where Kentucky is,
how to describe the wall of the Appalachian mountains
crumbling into the sweep of the turbulent Ohio River,
rushing west and south to the Mississippi? What should
the old man say: horses, hillbillies, bourbon, KFC, tobacco,
strip-mining coal from the sweet green belly of the earth?
None of these things hums or sings as the old man's soul
does when he thinks of his homeland.

He sputters against the clear air like a spotted bass
unable to form words. "Muhammad Ali," he finally spits,
"I live in the place where Muhammad Ali was born."
He raises his fists, squares his shoulders, does a
quick-step shuffle with his feet. He is aware he may
look faintly ridiculous standing there with his white beard
drifting in the breeze coming strong down Toomemägi,
channeling the Greatest Of All Time, chanting "Float like
a butterfly, sting like a bee..." but he thinks of Ali's power,
his poetry, oh! his beauty strength and grace, and he can
find no better way to communicate the vitality and spark of
where he comes from. The Estonian looks at the old man,
brow flickering puzzlement, and then his eyes light up.
"Yes! Yes!" he says, delighted. "Ali was against the war!

Ali refused the war!" and the old man thinks back to
May Day, 1971, remembers the shimmering distorted
images in the Reflecting Pool between the Washington
Monument and the Lincoln Memorial, phalanxes of police

marching against peaceful protestors, soldiers in riot gear
emerging from clouds of tear gas and pepper spray. He
feels again how his heart pounded hard as 12,614 were
arrested, herded and dragged battered and concussed
into vans, buses, panel trucks; he can still see the tanks
rolling in. He remembers how everything in him wanted
to run and the sudden calm washing down his spine, a
stubborn knowledge that he would never run from thugs
and bullies, no matter what uniform they wore, what
institution or power they claimed to represent. He stood
there, a young man old enough to be shipped to Vietnam,

thinking of 1964, when he and his brother tuned in to
those staccato bursts over the AM dial, nerves singing
as the Louisville Lip refused to go down before Sonny
Liston's brutal fists, kept dancing and punching even
when he couldn't see, taunting and hitting the great bear
where it hurt, over and over until the seventh round
when the giant sat down in the corner, utterly spent
and Cassius Clay, a young Black man from segregated
Louisville, Kentucky became World Heavyweight
Champion. And now, here in this city where memorials
are erected and destroyed and rebuilt with changing
tides of politics, cycles of oppression and freedom,
he thinks of Ali transforming to Cassius X and then
to Muhammad one-who-is-worthy-of-praise Ali

and how white men who'd made money on his back
cursed and reviled him when in 1966 he refused
the war publicly, "Man, I ain't got no quarrel with
them Viet Cong; no Viet Cong ever called me nigger."
And in the old man's young eyes, Ali became a

hero of those times, a shining legend, one of the
reasons he has spent his life traveling the world
fighting the many-headed serpent of hatred, fear
and oppression with his stories and poems. "Yes,"
he says, shaking hands heartily with the Estonian,
"Ali! Ali refused the war!" and the old man looks
into the stranger's eyes, sees the memory of
free speech suppressed, dissent punished, those
who disappeared, fate unknown, the exiles,
the ones who died fighting and for a long moment
they stand together, hands clasped across the
cobbled edge of Tartu's town square, each
understanding perfectly where the other comes from.

Soup Town Days

The blue and white graffiti on the alley wall reads
Kes kannatab, see kaua elab. "Do you have English?"
the old man asks a passerby. "Can you tell me what
this means?" The young woman he's stopped says,
"Of course! It is 'Who suffers the most, lives the longest,'"
and this is why the old man is thinking about suffering
as he follows the sound of singing down the steep hill
to the festival by the edge of the Emajõgi.

He has seen a poster pasted to a door and after puzzled
head-scratching deciphers *Supilinn* as "Soup Town."
He imagines he will find a crowd gathered around long
tables of deliciousness as Estonian mothers and grand-
mothers vie for medals—who has the best meat soup,
milk soup with pearl barley, herring stew, cabbage cream?
Won't he try this bread soup with its incense of apple and
cinnamon tickling his nose? The old man is ravenous;

he has been hungry for days now. Every backyard in Estonia
has a dozen fruit trees bursting into flower,
        long rows of carefully
pruned and trained raspberry canes, black currant bushes,
sandy earth tilled and frilled with strawberries, carrots, beets,
rhubarb, turnips and also tiny greenhouses with grapevines
snaking through the panes. As he hobbles down to Soup Town,
he admires an old, gnarled plum, tortured yet still flowering—
Just as I am, he thinks—surely this passion for growing food

is a remnant of the years of occupation. He imagines how
it was to queue through the long hours of the night, hoping
morning would bring bread, a packet of sugar, cooking oil
while the Soviets broke bountiful family farms apart, forced
collectivized farmers to grow according to plans drafted by
the uncalloused hands of bureaucrats and to sell at fixed prices.
Who is he to grumble in a land of plenty where thousands
died from malnutrition and the wisdom of the State?

There is something noble in suffering, something sacred.
He thinks of his own childhood in the farmlands of Kentucky,
how his mother would send him to pull corn or cucumbers
from fields of river-sweetened soil, how he'd creep down to
the cellar to retrieve a jar of pickles or beans from long shelves
ranged against starvation wages. His family knew how to
make do, carry on without complaint, and there was always
a little extra to help someone who suffered more than

they suffered. A good attitude and a bowl of soup shared?
Why, there was a double helping of salvation to beat back any
bad time. He remembers huddling in the cold dark attic over
the kitchen, wind whistling through the walls, listening to his
father tell a joke he'd heard at the coal mines to his mother,
her laughter bubbling up from below as she fried eggs for their
breakfast and the ragged rooster crowed the coming dawn.
To this day,he blesses his parents for showing him how
hard work and unrelenting humor feed endurance; nothing
can break him if he holds fast to joy. When he reaches the park
overlooking the Emajõgi, there is no soup.

People have spread blankets and sheets covered with used

books and toys, worn jeans, all for sale. He asks the man selling
ancient postcards, "Where is the soup?" and the man says, "Ah,
Soup Town is what we call this place. Poor people lived here
and had many gardens and each street is a food: Melon, Berry,
Pea, Potato. Mix streets together, make a good soup!"

He laughs and the old man laughs too. He sees the boy,
standing on a large wooden swing with ten others, sailing up
and down above a chattering, laughing crowd.
"You try külakiik?" the man says. "Every village has this swing.
It is important to swing together, have fun, yes?" Children
dressed as superheroes twirl folk dances before a stage
where fifty men and women sing in clear high harmony and the
audience sings along. Everyone must know all the words to
every song. A girl races past him, waving a torch which she

plunges into a huge pile of dry evergreen brush and the dusk
comes alive with towering fire. Showering sparks singe the old
man's face and he steps back into the shelter of the crowd.
He thinks of Buddha teaching that a man shot by pain's arrow
who responds with grief and laments, who beats his breast
in distress, shoots himself with a second arrow, this one
deep-piercing his mind; how a wise man understands it is only
the body suffering and refuses to let pain shatter his soul.
The old man has forgotten his hunger. His heart is humming,

drunk as bees in pollen time. It's time to swing,
it's time to sing, it is time to laugh in Soup Town
        where there is no soup yet the twisted trees in flower,
        each chorus sounding in the night, the fire itself breathes
Endure, Endure, Endure and you will triumph.

In the Temple of Words

"Cannot the tongue of this land,
In the wind of incantation,
Rising up to the heavens,
Seek eternity?" Kristjan Jaak Peterson

Krista Ojasaar invites the old man and the boy on
what turns out to be a two-hour private tour of the
vast historic Estonian Literary Museum. As they

start down the long corridor the old man says,
"Good lord, this place is huge. How many people
work here?" Krista says, "114, half are researchers."

Standing in the opulent hall, Krista shares the history
of the magnificent building, pointing out the intricately
laced and patterned wood work, designed by master

craftsmen, the gorgeous wallpaper, which looks like
it came right out of a castle from fairy lands, and then,
as they continue to weave in and out of rooms, with

researchers hard at work, she tells stories of the
ghosts who live here. She shares the story of a
young woman, The Lilac Lady, who hung herself.

Krista points to the big hook on the wall the woman
hung herself from. Krista tells stories of those who've
been frightened by the ghost, including the account of

one man who had stolen money from the museum.
The ghost appeared and scared the man so bad he
shot himself. Krista says, "He died right here." She

points to a spot on the floor directly in front of them and
the boy quick-steps back. They wind their way through
the rest of the first floor then head upstairs to view

portraits and photographs of Estonia's leading authors
then they wend down down deep down to the basement.
They come to a sudden stop in front of a stoutly locked

fireproof vault. Krista digs into her jacket pocket and
pulls out a huge rusty key, jiggles it into the keyhole
and with great effort unlocks the heavy steel door.

The old man helps her heave the door open. They step
into a dark room. Lights slowly brighten. The boy says,
"Wow!" as the room begins to glow and glistening glass

cases take shape. Krista says, "This is where we keep
the earliest handwritten Estonian manuscripts, the first
handwritten Bible translated into Estonian, handwritten

poems and letters by the patriarch of Estonian literature,
Kristjan Jaak Peterson, the matriarch of Estonian
literature, Lydia Koidula, by Friedrich Reinhold

Kreutzwald, author of our national epic, Kalevipoeg
son of Kalev, and so much more. This is the sacred
treasure chest of Estonian literature." The old man

mutters, "Holy, holy, holy! A city that knows wisdom is
more precious than rubies; nothing can compare to her,"
and they stand surrounded by words, the words that were,

the words that are, the unknown words that are yet to be
written but even now thrum in the livewire eccentric
stubborn practical mischievous spirits of Estonians

who flock to literary and music festivals, who sit quietly in
verdant wildflowered parks bathing in iridescent electric
orange and pink sunsets, the students who touch Kristjan

Jaak Peterson's statued feet to remember how young poets
can turn the established order upside down with language,
the women and men the old man's age who led a nation

to freedom through the power of poemed songs, and here
in the Estonian Literary Museum, in the precious literate
city of Tartu, the old man is filled with joy. He weeps

unabashedly, radiant tears of gratitude for the eternal
power of words and the gift of his calling. "I would be happy
to haunt this temple of words forever" he says, and the boy

quietly slips his hand into the old man's hand and says,
"Yes. A Kentucky ghost would be at home here," and
they walk to the glowing pages and, marveling, read.

Cheese & Thank You

The boy is sitting at a table in the garden outside the
Karl Ristikivi Muuseum, nose buried in Kalevipoeg.
The boy's Estonian is coming along quite nicely,
the old man thinks, while his? Hmmm. Not so much.

The old man is convinced there are hidden vowels
he cannot hear in every Estonian word. He asks how to
say this or that at the coffeehouse, in the grocery, repeats
what he hears as it is slowly offered in the tone reserved

for children, idiots and foreigners, and is met with frowns,
impatient corrections, or small tight smiles as heads
wag a discouraging "ei ei ei" his way. Here in a country
where that long-limbed poet Kristjan Jaak Peterson

sparked a national awakening of pride in things Estonian,
where stories and songs refused an occupying hegemony,
fueled the hunger for self-government, the right to exist
independently of Germany, Denmark, Sweden, Russia,

where Kristjan Jaak's statue on Toomemägi is garlanded
still with flowers, his birthday celebrated nationwide as
Mother Tongue Day, here the old man tries and tries
to get words right and is ashamed of his failure.

The old man sees En hand the boy a small plate. The boy
smiles and says "Juust." En smiles back approvingly.
Juust, the old man realizes, must mean "Thank you." He is

thrilled by this discovery. There is no better word to know

in any language and this is such a simple word even he
can say it: YOUst, YOUst. He rolls it over in his mouth.
What a lovely word; he cannot wait to use it! Later on,
the old man and the boy see the Estonian blues singer,

Kaisa Ling, who invites them to squeeze onto a bus
heading for the island of Saaremaa where she grew up.
"They're going to see a lake made by a meteor, butterflies,
Roman snails and two kinds of SEALS!" the boy exclaims

tugging the old man's sleeve. "Vikings were there! Please?"
and so they ride west, five hour by bus to Saaremaa.
As they climb out, Kaisa says, "Welcome. We are honored
that you came today; we look forward to visiting with you.

All of us are part of the Prima Vista literary festival; we are
hearing a lecture soon about the tradition of humor in writing.
I've heard from Kersti Unt and Doris Kareva that you are
considered a fine poet, a respected master of language."

The old man smiles, takes Kaisa's hands in his, kisses them
and intones "YOUst! YOUst!" while ecstatically beaming,
so pleased he can thank someone properly for their kindness.
Kaisa stares at him like he's lost his mind. The old man blushes

red then blue then purple, realizing he's said something wrong.
"Oh," he stutters. "I suppose
        YOUst does not mean 'Thank you'?"
Kaisa tilts her head to one side, regarding him poker-faced,
then politely says, "No. Juust is cheese. Juust is wonderful,

my favorite thing, but the word for thank you is aitäh." The old
man wants to crawl into a meteor crater and vanish.
"I'm sorry...." He trails off, miserable.
    "Would you say that word again?"
She does, three more times and each time he gives it a try

it is wrong, it is wrong, there is sound in there he cannot wrap
his mouth around. He wants to slink away, go for a walk on
the shore of the bay, get lost in a marsh or maybe wander into
the embrace of an angry brown bear. Anything but this.

"I think," Kaisa says, "perhaps you should stick with English."
She puts her arm around his shoulders. "Come inside. We will
talk about poetry and *you*? We'll fix *you* a snack." The boy says,
"Perhaps there's some juust?" "Yes, certainly juust," Kaisa says,

and before the old man can think twice, his mouth flies open
and he says "Aitäh." The boy grins. "Now you can say cheese
and thank you! A master of language, you are!" and there
in a room with huge windows overlooking a bay in Orissaare

on the northeastern edge of Saaremaa, they all laugh together.

The Uku Stone of Muhu Island

The old man hears Kaisa Ling whispering songs in his ear.
Kaisa has invited the old man and the boy for a journey,
what turns out to be a long long walk, to a sacred place.

Kaisa grew up here in Orissaare, a small community on
the northeastern tip of Saaremaa, Estonia's largest island.
They stop, near the shore, and look out upon the mist rising

from the gently rippling pink waters. Seagulls and eiders
sing praise songs to the new day. Kaisa is belting out old
blues songs, the ones sung by strong black women in

America's deep south. Standing by the bay, the old man
turns to Kaisa and says, "How old are you? I am 70." "29,"
she replies. The old man feels a trusting connection with

this young woman. Her soul rings ancient to his ear. He has
come to realize how important the question of trust is here
in Estonia so he falters and hesitates as he asks, "How in

the world did you come to know and be inspired by the
voices, the songs of American black women singing the
1920s blues? And you, you, now singing those heart

wrenching songs in Estonian and English. When did you
first hear the songs and what moved you to sing them as
if they are your own?" Kaisa stares deep and hard at the

old man, determining slowly but surely to trust him and
to share at least some of her truth with him. She says,
"I was christened here. I grew up here. This is my home.

I love this place and these people. I was a good girl, a
high achiever. I had many struggles, illnesses. I have
multiple sclerosis. I have been blessed with new

treatments and therapies. I am so thankful to be able to
walk." She pauses, then continues, "To be honest, it was
violence that brought me to the blues. I was in a very

difficult relationship with a much older rock musician for
too many years and I was extremely unhappy and afraid.
Then I found these blues songs that helped me find my

strength and these women who truly keep me upright.
I have always given credit to that man for giving me the
first thread of the tapestry but I was the one who took it and

ran with it. I have forgiven and forgotten, for sure. This is
why I feel such a strong connection to this music, why it
is so important to me. These songs are my autobiography

and the story of so many women in Estonia, in the States
and all over the world who have to endure this kind of life.
Saaremaa is a small community and talk spreads so fast.

When I was little I always knew who was being beaten at
home, knew when it happened. I hope it has changed and
will change even further. But I am also sure there are

women who feel my pain intimately when I sing." The old man suddenly sees himself a boy again, sleeping on his army cot, in the kitchen closet, his first bedroom. He has

pinned baseball pennants to the unfinished wood walls for decoration. He wakes up. His wind-up alarm clock reads 10pm. His Mama is standing at the other end of

the large closet ironing a waist-high pile of clothes. His Mama is always up way before sunrise, before anyone else, and she never gets to bed until long after the entire

family is asleep. He hates the way his Mama works her fingers to the bone and he despises how she is often treated badly, talked to wrong, by Daddy. In that moment, when he

was a boy, he decided he would always be on Mama's side, stand and fight for the good and fair treatment of all women. He knew then, as he has always known, that

women and men, girls and boys should be treated fair and equal. Kaisa guides the old man and the boy down a fairytale shaded lane lined by moss covered stones and

tall slender orange pines and silver birch climbing, reaching way high up into the blue Baltic sky. They cut through a farm with chickens and beehives and gorgeous

yellow flowers everywhere. The old man asks, "What kind of beautiful flower is this?" Kaisa smiles and plucks one. She eats the yellow flowers and offers flowers to the old man

and the boy. She says, "These are good for the bronchial
health. It is called cowslip. The Latin name is primula veris.
This is the most beloved wildflower of Estonia and has

been given some 200 names: swallow flower, golden key,
eye of the sky, flower of the maiden, rooster's pants,
coocoo paws." The old man mutters, "The poet's flower."

He plucks and eats two petals from his flower but saves
the other three petals and hands the flower to the boy saying,
"Here, let me press this between the pages of your

Kalevipoeg. I want to save it as a gift for my flower girl."
The boy hands him the book. He has nearly finished
reading it and carries it with him wherever he goes. They

leave the farm and enter a long field of clover, which
is surrounded by an old old stone fence. Kaisa says,
"Estonia has only two snakes, one is terribly poisonous,

the other is not poison. The poison snakes love to live in
the stone fences, including this one. There are many
stories in our folktales about the poison snakes, and

especially about the King Snake which appears every
spring, which is now." The boy, wide eyed, looks up at
Kaisa and says, "The King Snake?" She says, "Yes.

During winter the snakes all coil up together and in spring
they rise together as one. It is truly frightful to behold."
The boy cries, "For real?!" Kaisa says, "For real." The boy

says, "Woah! I think I'll stay off that fence!" Kaisa says,
"Look way down there, all the way across the field, nearly
to the end. See the giant stone, with the small tree growing

from it? That's where we're going. The end of our quest."
They take their time crossing the field of clover. Then, there
is the stone, the stone of all stones, the Uku Stone of Muhu

Island. The stone has craters, pockets of water, and small
crystals shimmering in the bright sunlight. The old man
notices shadowy stains. He wonders if they are blood

stains. Gifts have been placed on top the massive stone:
coins, flowers, metals, wood and stone carved into what
appear to be sacred objects, perhaps the animal totems

of an indigenous people. Kaisa says, "Once upon a time,
there were two of these stones, but one has vanished.
So this is the only remaining sacred stone. This is

the sacred Uku Stone of Muhu Island. It has
special powers. If anyone removes a gift they will be
sought out and punished. If anyone leaves a gift they

will be blessed. The stone was dedicated to the
deity Uku. It dates back thousands of years. In our
history it is associated with rituals, including blood

sacrifices. The Uku Stone bears witness to our
aboriginal religion of Estonia which is based on a
sustainable world view, humans being only one of

numerous animated beings. Even the stones are
alive. We are all children of Mother Earth." The old man
digs into his left front pocket and pulls out the leather

pouch he carries with him always. It holds many of
his sacred objects. He takes a blue crystal from the
pouch. When he was a boy, forever wandering the wild

nature backwoods of Kentucky, he found a small cave
on the side of a wooded hill. On the top of the hill was
a giant stone. He would often lie down on the stone and

stare up at the wind dancing through the trees, and the
blue sky and the dragon shaped clouds, and think about
traveling to foreign lands. In the cave he discovered a

cache of crystals. This is one. He holds it up over the
Uku Stone and says, "Thank you dear Uku Stone for
being here and for welcoming the boy and me. This gift

of blue crystal, which I have carried all my life, I present
to you now, by way of saying thank you. I honor and
respect all beings, all of life on our sacred Mother Earth.

Thank you." The old man bows, places the blue crystal
on the Uku Stone, and then the three of them turn and
walk back across the field of clover, their strides equal,

their hearts free, and Kaisa sings an old Ma Rainey tune
while the old man and the boy hum along in soft harmony.

The Lonely Black Storks of Estonia

"En," says the boy, seeking her in the greenhouse
where she's tucking larch cones into pots to sprout,
"En, what does this word mean in Estonian?" He points.
"Where did you get this, my boy?" En says, squinting
to bring the words into focus. "There's a pile of newspapers
in the museum," the boy replies. "I like the photos, see?"

He points to a fine photograph of a long lovely bird with a
bright red beak. "I think it's going to a party," the boy says.
"It's wearing an ebony coat and a white shirt and do you see
its pretty green and purple scarf? Is üksildus the word for
party?" En says, "It's a word for loneliness. This says
'The black storks of Estonia are suffering from loneliness.'"

The boy is shocked. "Why are they lonely? Don't they have
any friends?" "I don't think anyone knows for certain why
they are lonely," says En. "Their journeys grow harder as
the world changes. Places where storks could find a husband
or wife grow strange, unwelcoming. The ones that land where
they have always raised chicks look around and find no others

are there to say 'hello, won't you dance with me?'" The boy
shakes his head sadly. "That's a rotten awful story," he says.
"It is," says En. "In these weirding days, winds and weather
are shifting wildly. There are too many people revving engines,
slicking the seas with crude oil, cutting down trees to trade for
money, people paving over marshes, planting seeds coated in

poisons that kill the little bees, people digging caverns to bury
cities-full of sour trash, cheap things they craved that broke
long before they brought happiness. And nature? She cannot
keep her peace. Once she'd grumble or shake every 20 years,
she would flood cities once in a hundred years. But now? Every
day, every year she spasms and weeps. The black storks sit

lonesome on their empty nests and the rat kings are rising."
"Ah!" breathes the boy. "The old man said he'd tell me about
rat kings! Will you?" En sighs. "The winters grow colder in the
weirding days. The rats in winter huddle in heaps to survive;
their tails freeze and knot tight together. Twenty-three rats,
thirty-two rats with tails knotted tight. When spring comes,

the farmers find them, a twisted lump of suffering. The rats
cannot escape themselves; they have become one thing
and that thing is a harbinger of strange and painful times."
"What happens when rat kings rise?" the boy asks. "We have
a story," En frowns. "When people are greedy, when they
do not try to walk softly, when they no longer yearn to rest

forever in the hearts of forests, it is said the forests they spurn
will up their roots and leave. They will travel to where people
are still kind and make a little go a long way, where groves
are sacred, and mink, dormice and flying squirrels, wolf, lynx,
clans of bear and herds of elk, the hare, the fox and deer
can shelter and thrive." "And storks!" the boy exclaims.

"Storks too, my boy. Each creature needs a home and friends."
The boy imagines the earth groaning as giant conifers pull their
long roots away from her heart, her secret springs. It's a horrid
sound; it hurts his head to imagine it. He looks at En wanting

to hear her say no, it's just a story, but her steady gaze tells him it's the truth. He thinks about other photos in the newspaper:

the belly of a whale stuffed with plastic, a scrawny white bear drifting on a sliver of ice in a boiling sea. The boy quivers. "En, what if there are no good people left? What happens then? If the forests have no one left to care for them?" En hands him pine cones and a pot of black soil. "You will not let the earth die of loneliness, will you?" En says. "You will be her friend."

Transformations

The waning crescent moon sets; morning tiptoes in.
The boy has been sleeping in a nest of chair cushions
between cases that display old photos and letters
in the front room of the museum. Outside, a blackcap
merrily flutes its pre-dawn hymn to the coming sun.

The boy stretches—a long full stretch—and imagines
there is a wolf waking beside him. The wolf is stretching,
he is stretching. His muscles tingle; he feels strong
and good. Something has shifted in his body overnight.
The long bones of his legs ache pleasantly and there's

something stirring, something electric twitching to life
from the base of his spine through his belly and groin.
It's as if he has visited the underworld in his dreams,
swallowed a magic potion, and returned to this world
mid-transformation. "I think I'm becoming a wolf,"

he whispers to himself. "This happens in Estonia.
Perhaps I should sneak out and get a tattoo before
my body is covered with hair and tattoos are entirely
out of the question." The old man is covered in tattoos.
He's had most of them so long he forgets they're there

until he catches scarf-wearing old women, businessmen
staring at him. He wakes in the back room of the museum,
listens to the early train rattling in from Valga. He has made
a bed on the futon sofa where too many have sat; he's

laid it flat but still wakes prisoned in the deep crease.

He's been walking too much, and something's gone a bit
cattywampus in his left knee, what should be attached isn't.
In the gray crepuscular light, he imagines the burgundy
mattress enfolding him is her arms reaching him back
to her. "You've grown thin," he thinks she'd say. "You

should eat; you can't live on coffee and words, darling."
He imagines there are worse ways to go. It would be
grand to live on espresso with a brita kook now and then,
writing poem after poem until he was skin and bones
and everything he'd always wanted to say was said.

He would finally have time to sleep. "I could walk into
the woods," he thinks. "I'd curl up against a juniper,
inhale the spruce and larch. A scarred lame sinewy old
wolf with no words in the silence of the forest." And this
is how sunrise finds them in their separate corners of

the Karl Ristikivi Muuseum, each watchfully awake,
each quietly wondering what comes next.

The Museum of His Life

The boy is content squatting in the museum, has grown fond
of the pink stucco exterior with its metal plaque weeping
coppery stains to the earth, yet there are things he wants
to see. It seems possible to him that he can visit every wonder
the world has to offer and be back to the museum in time for
supper. On this day, he is clutching a glossy brochure.
"Let's go to the upside-down house!" He waves the slick paper
under the old man's tired eyes. "See! The house's roof balances
on the ground and inside? Everything is upside down!"
    He points.
There is a photograph of a man striding across the ceiling,
head barely clearing the dining table below, another of a child
doing a one-fingered handstand on a pink and white bed,
the tips of her toes brushing the pendant light above.

The old man has been writing a letter to the woman who loves
flowers. By his calculations, it is the 743rd note he has sent her.
He has not run out of things he wants to say. Today, he's been
remembering small details about her and writing these;
his page is scrawled with phrases that begin, "I love how you..."
He believes every inkwell in the world will run dry before he
reaches the end of words to remind her they are connected
still, even though the world itself divides them. He looks at
the boy standing in front of him, peers at the photographs
which, from where he sits, look exactly like what they are:
    people standing on floors made to look like ceilings.
He had a home once, filled with quilts and paintings. Instead of
blinds, he'd hung prisms from the curtain rods so the light of

the world spun rainbows 'round the walls of his rooms.

That is gone now and he is a temporary guest in a museum,
carrying all he owns in a backpack, waking each morning amid
cases of Karl Ristikivi's books, hand-lettered captions of faded
photos, yellowing letters, drafts of novels that fire, war, bombs
and rot decided to spare for a while longer yet. Time and again,
life has turned certainty in the future upside down, lifted him
when he was sure he was dying, lamed him when he felt strong.
He wonders what will remain when time is done with him,
whether anything he touched or loved or made will linger
100 years from now. Perhaps a few words he's typed will sing on
or flowers he planted will faithfully reseed each fall, rise again
in spring ? He doubts anyone will build a museum honoring his
peregrination across the planet and, really, would he want one?

Crazy to constrain the passion of a man's life, his dreams and
desires, mad imaginings and quiet hours, in glass-fronted cases
for the briefly curious to view. Better to vanish without a trace.
In that moment, he knows it is time to leave. He is finished;
it is time to go. He stuffs the unsigned letter into his backpack.
"Grab your book," he tells the boy. "We will pay our respects to
the upside-down house on our way out of town. And after that?
Who knows? It's time for us to move along." The boy grins.
Some magic, some wonderful experience waits wherever
they land, Estonia has proved that to him. And he?
He is willing to meet it, whatever, wherever it might be.
The old man locks the museum's door behind them,
hands the key to the boy. "Give this to En with our thanks
and a kiss from me." The boy races away.

It is a glorious spring afternoon in Tartu and the old man waits

patiently for the boy to return. He is content to watch blossoms
dance in the wind as swallows arrow back and forth from their
nests under the eaves, beaks laden with food for their young.
Inside the Karl Ristikivi Muuseum, his winter coat hangs
forgotten on the coat rack in the orange hall,
the only evidence that they once sojourned here.

May Day

Every hour, we take our lives into our hands and journey on.

The old man believes she is somewhere still.
    Perhaps this world,
perhaps one parallel, a world of sirens or deep silence,
    he cannot tell.
He floats 30,000 feet above a sleeping world with his eyes shut,
imagining he is going home to the woman who loves flowers.

The boy sits cross-legged in the seat beside him, remembering
En's hands on his shoulders as they said goodbye. "There are
many ways life will surprise you," she said. "Some things you
can fight, some you'll find a way to fix, some you must accept

just as they are." He handed her the key to the museum and as
she took it, it changed into a rook feather. "The important bit,"
she said, as she tucked the feather into his wild curling hair,
"is to never allow big-eyed fear to lead you away from freedom.

Don't forget that when the storms come, when everything is
crazed with lightning, when thunder shakes you. Nägemist!
I'll see you soon!" And then she vanished. The old man stood
waiting silently at the edge of the orchard, and they were off,

leaving Estonia for lands unknown in the belly of a humming
aluminum butterfly. When the plane suddenly bucks and dives
the first time, it is fun—*just like a roller coaster*, the boy thinks,
Whee!—but the second turbulent spin sends his stomach

95

whizzing toward his throat and the Indian girl across the aisle begins to cry and it's not fun anymore. The old man bolts up from his dream of the woman clad in daisies dancing through fields in the land of his birth and blessing. The boy looks for

a reassuring sign in the old man's eyes, but finds only panic. The boy imagines he can feel the invisible pilot before them, fighting the turbulent winds on their behalf, heroic muscles straining to wrench them up, down, any which way to safety.

He is terrified. He does not want to fall out of the sky tonight, the upside-down house was closed when they left town and he'd promised himself to return one day to see it. He wants to live forever and as he thinks this, his terror changes to deep

grief: he might never see the wolf or the crows again, he might never plant the tree a black stork will raise her chicks in, never glimpse the ghost of the Lilac Lady or taste lemon tea or tuck the ogre's lunch under a silver tub at the edge of the garden.

Just as he thinks this sadness is too much to bear, he realizes he cannot hear the plane's engines. It is as if everything outside the cabin has disappeared as En had disappeared, even the winds have melted away and the plane hangs suspended by

the slim silver line of the moon, to plummet or to rise as fate sees fit. He can hear passengers weeping quietly around him, the old man's breathing staggers and jumps, but a deep calm suddenly rises inside the boy; it starts at his toes, he can feel

it flowering and flowing through his every capillary, soothing,
carrying with it echoes of joy: Chango spray-painting a mural,
Jaan's booming bass-laced poetry, Marja smoothing Greta's
hair, Hilary sweet-talking the bookstore's cat, and the old man

Oh! how he's understood the boy's heart before he himself did.
He reaches over and takes the old man's hand, holds on tight.
He doesn't know where the words come from, but they are the
only words he can say as they hang in fate's balance, "Love

surrounds us, love supports us, love will carry us through,"
the only words that can possibly matter when the known world
has evanesced and no one knows how the story ends. "We
are safe in love's hands, love is here, love is everywhere,"

and he opens his heart to the universe, full of trust, believing.

Afterword

In a truly collaborative work, it quickly can become difficult to pinpoint "who wrote what." Some of these poems were written when the two poets were far apart—Ron in Tartu, Estonia, Jinn in Clarksville, Indiana. Others were written during our ten days together in Estonia. We worked on many poems together in real time: using Facebook's video chat to read drafts and discuss, using Google Docs' power to inhabit the pages together in the same moment, each watching the other type and erase, adding comments, questions and suggestions in helpful sidebar conversations. Other poems were our gift to the other to find when waking from the seven hour time difference that divided us. The act of writing became a way to connect with each other even as we deliberately, deeply, emotionally connected to Estonia itself. There is not a single work in this book that was not touched or influenced by the other poet's experience, stories, questions, feelings, wonderment or keyboard.

That said, we have attempted to roughly sketch who wrote what in the list of poems below, as well as indicate which "Night at the Museum" each poem represents.

1.   Blessed Are the Innocent: (LEAVING FOR ESTONIA: 01 Apr; written by Jinn with edits by Ron)
2.   Temporal Nonlocality (FIRST NIGHT OVER THE ATLANTIC OCEAN: 01/02 Apr; written by Jinn with edits by Ron)
3.   On Luck and Magic (SECOND NIGHT: 02/03 Apr; originally sketched by Ron, rewritten by Jinn with elaboration, final edits by Ron)

4. The Ghost of Karl Ristikivi (THIRD NIGHT: 03/04 Apr; first & third stanzas written mostly by Ron with edits by Jinn, second stanza written by Ron (first half)/Jinn (second half), final stanza written by Jinn)

5. In the Ruins (FOURTH NIGHT: 04/05 Apr; first half written mainly by Ron, second half written mainly by Jinn, heavy cross-over of editing in this one)

6. The Ogre's Lunch (FIFTH NIGHT: 05/06 Apr; drafted by Ron, rewritten and elaborated by Jinn, edited by Ron)

7. What the Old Man Sees Upstairs (SIXTH NIGHT: 06/07 Apr; first 2 ½ stanzas mainly written by Ron, second 2 ½ stanzas mainly written by Jinn)

8. The Wolf at the Door (SEVENTH NIGHT: 07/08 Apr; written by Jinn with edits by Ron)

9. The Monsters (EIGHTH NIGHT: 08/09 Apr, original sketch and early draft by Ron, reworked & elaborated by Jinn, final edits by Ron)

10. When Everything Blossoms (NINTH NIGHT: 09/10 April; written mainly by Jinn, second stanza by Ron)

11. Midnight on Toome Hill (TENTH NIGHT: 10/11 April; written by Ron with edits by Jinn)

12. Words Worth Dying For (ELEVENTH NIGHT: 11/12 April; written by Jinn with edits by Ron)

13. Taking out the Trash (TWELFTH NIGHT: 12/13 April; initial sketch by Ron, main writing by Jinn, final edits by Ron)

14. The Language of Angels (THIRTEENTH NIGHT: 13/14 April; written by Ron)

15. On the Terrible Loneliness of Heroes (FOURTEENTH NIGHT: 14/15 April; written by Jinn)

16. The Kentucky Lion (FIFTEENTH NIGHT: 15/16 April; written by Ron with edits by Jinn)

17. The Angel's Bridge (SIXTEENTH NIGHT: 16/17 April; written by Jinn)

18. The Illusion of Choice (SEVENTEENTH NIGHT: 17/18 April; written by Jinn)

19. The Old Man is Kicked out of Church (EIGHTEENTH NIGHT: 19/20 April; written by Ron with the bit about the service at the Virgin with Three Hands Church adapted by Ron from writing by Jinn)
20. The Field Guide (NINETEENTH NIGHT: 20/21 April; written by Jinn)
21. The Magic of Rejection (TWENTIETH NIGHT: 21/22 April; written by Jinn with edits by Ron)
22. The Cathedral of Crows (TWENTY-FIRST NIGHT: 22/23 April; first draft written by Ron, edited, elaborated and rewritten by Jinn)
23. Homeland (TWENTY-SECOND NIGHT: 23/24 April; written by Jinn, based on stories Ron shared with an audience in Tartu about his experiences as a young man and an encounter between Ron and an Estonian stranger that Jinn witnessed)
24. Soup Town Days (TWENTY-THIRD NIGHT: 24/25 April; written by Jinn)
25. In the Temple of Words (TWENTY-FOURTH NIGHT: 25/26 April; written by Ron with some rewriting by Jinn in the final third of the poem)
26. Cheese & Thank You (TWENTY-FIFTH NIGHT: 26/27 April; written by Jinn with a few edits by Ron)
27. The Uku Stone of Muhu Island (TWENTY-SIXTH NIGHT: 27/28 April; written by Ron with a few edits by Jinn)
28. The Lonely Black Storks of Estonia (TWENTY-SEVENTH NIGHT: 29/30 April; written by Jinn based on mutual musing about whether there were storks in Estonia and a surprising headline in Google's first return and the conversations that followed)
29. Transformations (TWENTY-EIGHTH NIGHT: 30/31 April; written by Jinn)
30. The Museum of His Life (TWENTY-NINTH NIGHT: 31 April/01 May; written by Jinn with the idea to leave the old

Thank You

The authors gratefully thank the people of both Tallinn and Tartu, Estonia for their spirit, stories, voices, songs and hospitality so freely shared with two sojourners in their midst. While it is impossible to thank everyone by name, we would be remiss if we did not mention:

- **Al Paldrok** and **Diverse Universe** for introducing Ron to Estonia in 2012.
- **Ann Marvet**, editor of the journal *Estonian Nature* and a member of the Estonian Commission for Nature Conservation, for sharing her lovely garden outside the Karl Ristikivi Muuseum, her passion for the care and preservation of the planet, and for unknowingly birthing the wise-woman character En in this collection.
- **Arne Merilai** for the interaction that led to the poem "The Kentucky Lion."
- **Berk Vaher, Marja Unt, Kerstin Vestel, Siim Lill, Kaisa Ling**, and the entire **Insomniacathon Production Team** for helping Ron produce Estonia's first ever 24-hour non-stop music & poetry Insomniacathon, at The Tartu Literary House, to conclude the 2019 Prima Vista International Literature Festival.
- **Doris Kareva** for her friendship, her heroic, inspiring poetics, the gift of her translation of these poems to Estonian, and her shared experience as a poet and activist during a time of oppression and repression which informs our poem "Words Worth Dying For."
- **Hannes Ots** aka **Chango** for the interaction that led to the poem "Hometown" and for mysteriously appearing hither

and yon at just the right moments, reinforcing our belief in quantum physics.

- **Hilary Bird** for her walking tour of Tartu, her pioneering fascinating book "Introduction to Estonian Literature", her laughter and stories, friendship and help with both pronunciation and printing.
- **Jaan Malin** for his strong and beautiful voice sharing poem and song and his warm friendship.
- **Kaisa Ling** for meeting Ron at the airport upon his arrival to Estonia and delivering him to the Tartu bus, as well as the gift of the blues sung in Estonian, and an amazing visit to Saaremaa, the island where she grew up. What beauty!
- **Kaisa Ling, Andy Willoughby, Kalle Niinikangas, Amir Darwish, Aapo Ilves, Eerik Kokk, Erki-Andres Nuut, Steve Vanoni, Agnese** and **Madara Rutkēviča,** and **Ellips** for performing with Ron at Insomniacathon.
- To the ghost of **Karl Ristikivi**, whose "Night of Souls" harmonizes with our own imagined journey through a place where time and space are distorted and the unsettlingly fantastic is not only possible but probable.
- **Kersti Unt** for her delightful conversations and insight into Estonian history and culture.
- **Krista Ojasaar** for the two-hour private tour of the Estonian Literary Museum that led to the poem "In the Temple of Words."
- **Lilian Mengel** for her wonderful photographs, as well as outstanding graphic design work on the Insomniacathon and Prima Vista Festival posters and programs.
- **Madara** and **Agnese Rutkēviča** for translating Ron's "The Storm Generation Manifesto" into Latvian and for performing it with him at the Insomniacathon.
- **Maigi Lokka** and **Ruth Pärnaku** at the Tartu City Hall Information Center for their friendly help in getting Ron's feet on the ground by providing maps, directions, and event info.

- **Marja Unt** for doing a magnificent job as coordinator for the Writer in Residence program and helping Ron in many ways during his tenure, as well as for the invitation to Supilinna Päevad 2019 that led to "Soup Town Days."
- *Müürileht* and **Maarja Pärtna** for the feature article on Ron, 5/08/19.
- **Siim Lill**, owner of Utoopia Bookstore, for hosting Ron's first Tartu reading/talk with Hilary Bird, and for stocking Ron's books and CDs.
- *Sirp* and **Doris Kareva** for the feature article on Ron, 5/10/19.
- The good folks at the **Tallinn HeadRead Literary Festival** for welcoming Ron and Jinn in 2014.
- **Uku Uusmees,** assistant manager at Tallinn Airport, for meeting Ron at the gate when he landed in Estonia
- Deep respect and countless thank yous to the **UNESCO/Tartu City of Literature Writer in Residence Selection Committee: Berk Vaher, Marja Unt, Janika Kronberg, Krista Ojasaar**. The work you do to make Tartu a worldwide leader in literature is a treasure beyond measure. Kui suurepärane õnnistus see küll on!

Additional thanks to heroes closer to home:

- Our dear friend and neighbor **Angie Rice Vittitow** for enduring draft readings of poems that don't rhyme and for traveling with Jinn to Estonia
- **Howard and Nancy Bruner Wilson** for their faithful friendship and support
- **Monica Stewart** for her brilliant, inspiring artwork
- **Roz Newman, Rani Whitehead** and **Becky Massey** for holding down the fort in Jinn and Angie's absence
- To our parents—**Edwin and Greta Whitehead, Rodney and Joan Walter Fuller**—who encouraged our love of stories, poems and songs by sharing their own love of

literature with us early and often. You planted beautiful seeds in us "once upon a time" and made sure they grew. Thank you.

About the Authors

Kentucky-born poet, writer, editor, publisher, scholar, activist **Ron Whitehead** is the author of 30 books and 40 cds.

He has performed thousands of shows, with musicians and bands, round the world. He has produced over 3,000 poetry & music events, festivals, and non-stop 24 & 48 & 72 & 90 hour Insomniacathons throughout Europe and the USA.

He has published over 2,000 titles including works by Jack Kerouac, Allen Ginsberg, William S. Burroughs, Neal Cassady, Lawrence Ferlinghetti, Gregory Corso, Herbert Huncke, David Amram, Diane di Prima, Amiri Baraka, Ed Sanders, Anne Waldman, Hunter S. Thompson, Andy Warhol, Yoko Ono, Jim Carroll, Bono, Robert Hunter, Lee Ranaldo, Frank Messina, Birgitta Jonsdottir, Douglas Brinkley, E. Ethelbert Miller, Michael Dean Odin Pollock, Jan Kerouac, John Updike, Rita Dove, Eithne Strong, Theo Dorgan, President Jimmy Carter, Seamus Heaney, Thomas Merton, Robert Lax, Edvard Munch, Knut Hamsun, Jean Genet, James Laughlin, Brother Patrick Hart, Wendell Berry, His Holiness The Dalai Lama and many others. He wrote the poem Never Give Up with The Dalai Lama.

When not traveling the world he home bases at his hermitage on Cherokee Road in the Highlands of Louisville, Kentucky. You can contact Ron through his website: www.tappingmyownphone.com or by email: ronwhiteheadpoet@gmail.com.

Jinn Bug is a poet, photographer, gardener, activist, visual artist and life-long dreamer. She was born in Baltimore, Maryland where she spent her childhood memorizing poems, sticking her nose in a succession of books and trying to figure out the difference between lying and fiction. She rambled her way first to Louisville, Kentucky and then across the mighty Ohio River to historic Clarksville, Indiana. Her photography, vignettes and poems have appeared in Appalachian Heritage, New Southerner, LEO Weekly, Fiolet & Wing—An Anthology of Domestic Fabulism, Aquillrelle, For Sale, Pure Uncut Candy, The Rooted Reader, Gyroscope Review and other print and virtual publications. You can visit her at www.JinnBug.com or reach her through email at onliestjinn@gmail.com.

A bilingual Estonian/English edition of this book was published by Puhas Leht in Tartu, Estonia in November 2020 as "ÖÖD MUUSEUMIS ehk Lood Kentucky Vana Mehe ja tema lähedaste seiklustest Tartus ja Eestis", translation by poet Doris Kareva.

About the Translator

Doris Kareva *is a poet, translator and editor, and a Tartu University alumna. She has published poetry, essays and short prose, translated world classics (Akhmatova, Auden, Beckett, Brodsky, Brontë, Dickinson, Gibran, Kabir, Rumi, Shakespeare, etc.) and compiled anthologies.*

Doris Kareva's poetry has been translated into over 20 languages, it has often been set into music, staged and performed in Estonia and abroad.

About the Illustrator

Monica Stewart is a multimedia artist working primarily with paper. She received her BFA from Murray State University and her MFA in Studio Art at the University of Louisville. Making work that explores the relationship between narrative and object, she often draws on abject imagery from fairy tales to allude to female agency, the magical, and the grotesque. You can view more of Monica's work at www.monica-stewart.com.